The Story of Us

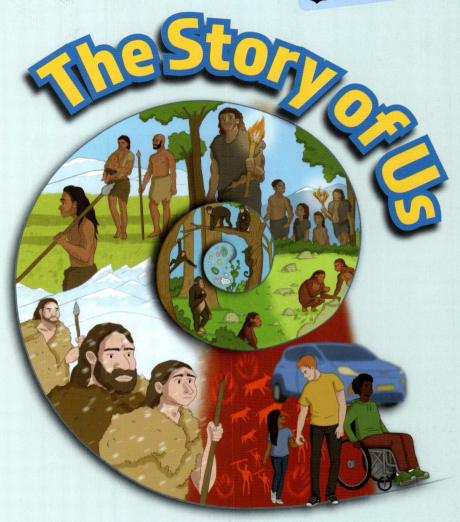

Written by Emily Hibbs

Illustrated by Dan Widdowson

RISING STARS

Hachette UK's policy is to use papers that are natural, renewable and recyclable products and made from wood grown in well-managed forests and other controlled sources. The logging and manufacturing processes are expected to conform to the environmental regulations of the country of origin.

ISBN: 9781398325746

Text, Illustrations, design and layout © Hodder and Stoughton Ltd
First published in 2022 by Hodder & Stoughton Limited (for its Rising Stars
imprint, part of the Hodder Education Group),
An Hachette UK Company
Carmelite House, 50 Victoria Embankment, London EC4Y 0DZ
www.risingstars-uk.com

Impression number 10 9 8 7 6 5 4 3 2 1

Year 2026 2025 2024 2023 2022

Author: Emily Hibbs
Series Editor: Tony Bradman
Commissioning Editor: Hamish Baxter
Illustrator: Dan Widdowson/Bright International C
Educational Reviewer: Helen Marron
Design concept and layouts: Lorraine Inglis
Editor: Amy Tyrer

With thanks to the schools that took part in the dev ... y School, Ancaster; Downsway Primary School, Reading; Fer ... lough; Griffin Park Primary School, Blackburn; St Barnabas CE First & ... and Wilton CE Primary School, Wilton.

The publishers would like to thank the following fo ...

p4-5, 54-56©eakgaraj/Adobe Stock; p4©millaf/Ado ... e Stock; p6©Engdao/Adobe Stock; henk bogaard/Adobe Sto ... be Stock; Ronnie Howard/Adobe Stock; Globus 60/Adobe Stock; arro ... , Adobe Stock; luca lopez/EyeEm/Adobe Stock; Jacob Lund/Adobe Stock; p7©bimserd/Adobe Stock; ch.krueger/Adobe Stock; Abeselom Zerit/Adobe Stock; Robert Kneschke/Adobe Stock; luismolinero/Adobe Stock; Ourteam/Adobe Stock; p8©Science History Images/Alamy Stock Photo; hstiver/Adobe Stock; Dennis/Adobe Stock; Grispb/Adobe Stock; Tobias/Adobe Stock; p9©The History Collection/Alamy Stock Photo; VectorMine/Adobe Stock; p11©nickolae/Adobe Stock; Don Paulson/Alamy Stock Photo; p12-17, 42-49©popaukropa/Adobe Stock; p13©Steffen Foerster/Shutterstock; marcel/Adobe Stock; milkovasa/Adobe Stock; Cheattha/Adobe Stock; p14©Brum/Shutterstock; Microgen/Adobe Stock; thananya_k/Adobe Stock; p15©PLG/Adobe Stock; sparkerphotos/Adobe Stock; p15, 21, 33, 38©stockdevil/Adobe Stock; p16©Radu Razvan/Adobe Stock; Chip Somodevilla/GettyImages; p17©fizzgig/Adobe Stock; BillionPhotos.com/Adobe Stock; Emilia Stasiak/Adobe Stock; Eric Isselée/Adobe Stock; p18-23©brandianna/Adobe Stock; p18©vectorpocket/Adobe Stock; Diego Barucco/Shutterstock; ssstocker/Adobe Stock; p19©pict rider/Adobe Stock; Catmando/Shutterstock; p20©Minden Pictures/Alamy Stock Photo; Maciej Czekajewski/Adobe Stock; p21©Uryadnikov Sergey/Adobe Stock; p22©Visual Generation/Adobe Stock; p23©Danny Ye/Shutterstock; p24-29, 36-41©PavloArt/Adobe Stock; p24©pandavector/Adobe Stock; spiritofamerica/Adobe Stock; Oleg Znamenskiy/Adobe Stock; p25©Clifford Ling/ANL/Shutterstock; National Geographic Society/Smithsonian Institution; Durova/WikiImages; p26©AFP/Stringer/GettyImages; Sabena Jane Blackbird/Alamy Stock Photo; World History Archive/Alamy Stock Photo; p27©REUTERS/Alamy Stock Photo; agefotostock/Alamy Stock Photo; p28©Danita Delimont/Alamy Stock Photo; World History Archive/Alamy Stock Photo; p29©Cro Magnon/Alamy Stock Photo; WH_Pics/Adobe Stock; p30©ssstocker/Adobe Stock; THOMAS & PAT LEESON/SCIENCE PHOTO LIBRARY; Vladimir Wrangel/Shutterstock; Liam Bunce/Alamy Stock Photo; rai/Adobe Stock; p31©The Natural History Museum/Alamy Stock Photo; PRISMA ARCHIVO/Alamy Stock Photo; p33©Enrique/Adobe Stock; Ique Perez/Shutterstock; Vikivector/Adobe Stock; WH_Pics/Adobe Stock; p34©Danny Ye/Shutterstock; p35©dimamoroz/Adobe Stock; Ariane Citron/Adobe Stock; p36©picture-waterfall/Adobe Stock; kotjarko/Adobe Stock; prochym/Adobe Stock; p39, 54©Roger Cracknell 01/classic/Alamy Stock Photo; p39©STR/Stringer/GettyImages; pyty/Adobe Stock; p41©UPI/Alamy Stock Photo; p42©deagreez/Adobe Stock; p43©jim/Adobe Stock; Krakenimages.com/Adobe Stock; p46©Jazmine/Adobe Stock; serikbaib/Adobe Stock; Brent Hofacker/Adobe Stock; wirojsid/Adobe Stock; p47©Andrea Izzotti/Adobe Stock; p49©auntspray/Adobe Stock; Catmando/Adobe Stock; p50-53©tampatra/Adobe Stock; p50©whiteMocca/Shutterstock; p51©Pormezz/Adobe Stock; p52©Elnur/Shutterstock; p53©lobodaphoto/Adobe Stock; Richard Carey/Adobe Stock; Soloviova Liudmyla/Shutterstock; Romolo Tavani/Adobe Stock.

MIX
Paper from responsible sources
FSC
www.fsc.org
FSC™ C104740

A catalogue record for this title is available from the British Library.

Printed in India.

Orders: Please contact Hachette UK Distribution, Hely Hutchinson Centre, Milton Road, Didcot, Oxfordshire, OX11 7HH.
Telephone: (44) 01235 400555. Email: primary@hachette.co.uk.

Contents

Hello, Human

You are part of an amazing group of animals. We build skyscrapers stretching up to the clouds and paint wonderful works of art. We speak complicated languages and share powerful stories. We have travelled all over our planet and have even gone beyond, shooting off into space to explore further. But how did we get here? Where did we come from?

Ten million years ago, there wasn't a single human on this planet. Today, there are over seven billion of us. We got here like every other creature on Earth – through millions of years of evolution. Evolution is how animals change and develop over time.

You might have seen a picture like this before. It shows an ape evolving into a human being, in a neat, straight line.

Human evolution however, didn't happen in a neat line, but like a big, branching tree. The branches split off in different directions, with some leading to dead ends. Finally, along one branch, modern humans evolved, see below just some of the humans from that branch.

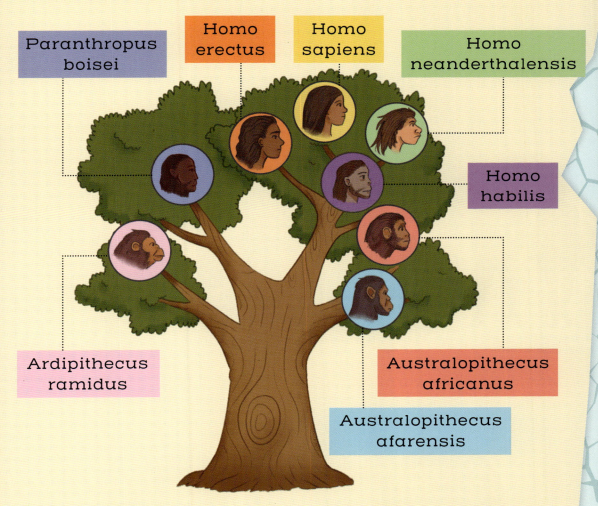

Paranthropus boisei

Homo erectus

Homo sapiens

Homo neanderthalensis

Homo habilis

Ardipithecus ramidus

Australopithecus africanus

Australopithecus afarensis

Today, we are the only humans on Earth. However, different kinds of humans have lived on this planet in the past. In this book, you can find out about some of the ancient animals and early humans we might have evolved from. They are known as our **ancestors**. You can discover how they changed, or **adapted**, over time to survive in their surroundings. You'll learn their stories and marvel at the mystery of what became of them.

1 What Are We?

All animals, including humans, fit into groups.
Animals are put into groups because they might look
similar or their bodies might work in a similar way.
Here are some of the groups modern humans fit in to.

We are mammals!

Mammals have warm blood. They can have hair or fur and they
make milk for their babies.

We are primates!

Primates are a group of mammals with
eyes on the front of their heads and
fingers that can grasp hold of things.

We are great apes!

Great apes are a smaller group of primates, which includes humans, chimpanzees, gorillas and orangutans. Great apes have no tails, flexible thumbs and are pretty clever. Humans are the smartest of all the great apes.

A special name

Every type of animal on the planet has a special scientific name. The scientific name for modern humans is **Homo sapiens**. *Homo* means 'human' and *sapiens* means 'clever', so our name means 'clever human'.

How did we get here?

Most people used to believe that human beings had always existed, since the beginning of time. They thought we were created looking and acting just as we do now. They thought we had always worn clothes, spoken complicated languages and used tools. Some people still believe this. However, most scientists now think that humans have been through lots of changes. The way those changes have happened is through evolution.

So, what is this evolution thing anyway? And why does it matter? To understand evolution, we must start with a man named Charles Darwin …

All about evolution

Charles Darwin was a scientist who lived in the 19th century. As a little boy, he used to collect all sorts of interesting items, from birds' eggs to beetles. When he was grown up, he set out on an adventure aboard a ship called HMS *Beagle*. The ship took Darwin to South America and Australia. He made notes about all the different kinds of animals and plants he found there.

He noticed that living things seemed to be suited to their surroundings. Often, animals living in hot, dry places could go a long time without water. Animals living in trees sometimes had colours or patterns that helped them blend in. He wondered how this could happen. Could animals adapt to their **habitats**?

Dear Diary,

Today I noticed something about the little brown birds living on these South American islands.
They look alike, but they have different shaped beaks on different islands.

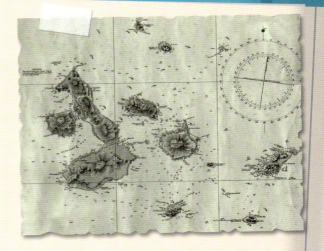

On one island they have long beaks. They eat insects.

On another, they have little beaks. They eat fruit.

And on another, they have sharp beaks. They peck at tough cacti.

I think that, long ago, all these birds looked the same. Over time, their beaks changed depending on what food was available on their island. I've got an idea about how this might have happened …

Darwin wrote a book about his discoveries. In it, he explained how animals could evolve over time to look and act differently. Here's how it works …

Imagine a group of beetles living in a forest. The beetles are exactly the same, except some are red and some are green.

Birds are the beetles' **predators**. They hunt for beetles to eat. The red beetles are easier to spot than the green beetles, which blend in with the leaves. The birds snap up more of the red beetles.

More of the green beetles survive. They live longer and have more babies. They pass on their colour to their babies, so more green beetles are born than red beetles.

As time goes on, more and more green beetles are born. The birds still need to eat though, and they still find some of the beetles. The beetles that blend in best are most likely to survive and have babies.

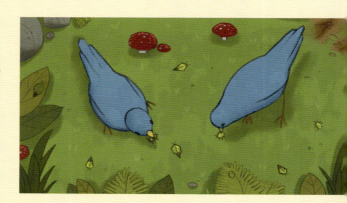

Over the years, the green beetles start to look more like the leaves they hide among. They have evolved to have the best chance of survival.

← This kind of defence is called camouflage.

To start with, people were shocked by the thought of evolution. But as more evidence was discovered, like the **fossils** you'll find in this book, most people began to accept Darwin's ideas. They realised that, over time, evolution could be much more dramatic than changing beaks or beetle colours. Over millions of years, animals could transform from one creature into a completely different one. For example, some types of dinosaurs evolved into today's birds!

↑ Charles Darwin

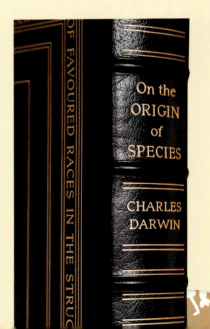

Of all the animals alive on Earth today, modern humans are most similar to chimpanzees. We did not evolve from chimpanzees, but, long ago, the ancestors of both chimpanzees and humans evolved from the same animal.

← Darwin's book about evolution

2 Stones and Bones

We can find out about evolution through fossils. Many animals that have evolved are now extinct, which means there are none left alive on our planet. We know about these ancient animals, from dinosaurs to early humans, because of what they left behind. Living things rot away when they die, and most leave no trace. But sometimes conditions are just right to leave a fossil. A fossil is the remains of ancient life – or the marks left by it.

Here's one way fossils are formed...

STEP 1	STEP 2

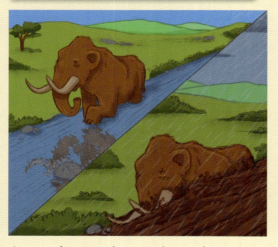

An animal dies. It is quickly buried by little bits of solid material, called sediment. The sediment could be ash from a volcano or mud and sand carried by water.

The soft bits of the animal's body, like its fur, skin and organs, rot away. This leaves behind the hard bits of its body, such as the skeleton, made up of its bones and teeth. Pressure causes the sediment to form into rock around the skeleton.

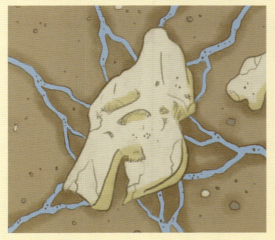

Bits of the skeleton are worn away by water seeping through the rock. Tiny, solid crystals in the water, called minerals, fill the gaps. Sometimes, these minerals replace all the bone and turn into bone-shaped rocks. Sometimes, some of the real bone remains.

The fossil stays hidden in the rock, until it is dug up. Occasionally, water or wind wear away the rock to reveal the fossil.

The bodies of most ancient animals rotted or were munched on by predators, so they never ended up as fossils.

Fossil finders

People who study our past are called archaeologists. Their aim is to understand what humans' lives were like long ago by looking at the things they left behind. Archaeologists visit sites where fossils might be found and carefully dig into the rock. As well as bones, they look for other things, including ancient tools and cave art.

← Rock is formed in layers, with the oldest rock at the bottom. The further down you go, the older the fossils you find.

Putting together a fossil is tough. Mostly, archaeologists find the odd bone here and there, rather than a whole skeleton. They must make a note of every tiny bit of bone they find. Then they try to fit them together. It's like a very tricky jigsaw puzzle!

Studying fossils

Fossils can tell us a lot about a creature. Leg bones can let us know whether an animal climbed trees or ran across open grassland. Teeth can share secrets about what an animal ate. Skull size might suggest how big an animal's brain was, which helps us guess how clever it was.

↑ Woolly rhinoceros skull

← A dinosaur fossil

Fossil Fact File

Name: *Australopithecus africanus*
(say: aw–struh–loh–pith–uh–cus a–free–kaa–nus)

Lived: 3.2 to 2 million years ago

This is a fossil of an early human skull. It was discovered in South Africa in 1924. Archaeologists can tell a lot from this fossil. For example, because it still has some baby teeth, they know the skull belonged to a child who was between two to three years old.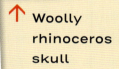

One way scientists can tell the age of a fossil is by working out the age of the rock it was stuck in.

Today, we have lots of technology to help us understand what fossils should look like. We can create 3D images on computers and compare them to the skeletons of living animals and other fossils we've found. This can help us create amazing images of our extinct ancestors!

There are ways we can find out even more about fossils than just looking at them on the outside. We can study them on the inside, too. Scientists can scan fossils to create computer images of them. In fossils where bits of real bone or teeth remain, we can look at the **DNA**.

← Scientist 3D scanning a dinosaur leg bone

What is DNA?

DNA is found in every single living thing. It's contained in every part of your body: your hair, your blood, your skin and even your spit! But it's so tiny you can't see it with your eyes. DNA contains information about how a living thing will look and act. It affects things such as hair colour and height.

↑ A computer model of DNA.

By looking at DNA, scientists can work out which animals are closely related. The more closely related an animal is, the more similar its DNA. For example, we share 98% of our DNA with chimpanzees. We only share 65% with sharks.

All living things share some DNA, from flowers to flies to foxes. This is because we all evolved from the same early living things. To find out about that, we have to go back a really long way – right back to the start of our story.

3 Back to the beginning

Earth formed about 4.5 billion years ago. For millions of years, it didn't look much like the planet we know today, but a big fireball. Eventually, things cooled down and the land and oceans formed.

Early life

Living things first showed up in Earth's oceans about 3.8 billion years ago. To begin with, living things were simple and very tiny – so tiny you wouldn't have been able to see them! They stayed like that for a long time, but then things slowly began to change.

Some of those tiny living things evolved into the first plants, and some into the first animals. By 530 million years ago, the first fish were darting through Earth's oceans. Living things evolved again and again, until countless creatures walked, swam, scuttled and flew across the planet.

The first primates evolved more than 80 million years ago. They were small and mouse-like. They lived in trees and tried to keep out of the way of bigger, scarier animals, like the dinosaurs.

About 66 million years ago, a huge space rock, called an asteroid, smashed into the planet. Its impact caused most of the dinosaurs to die out, along with 75% of life on Earth.

Among the survivors were some of those little primates. They had big brains for their size and could adapt to their surroundings. They didn't need much food to get by, which was lucky, as the asteroid impact had wiped out lots of food sources.

Our ancient ancestors → might have looked a bit like this primate.

Fossil Fact File

Name: *Purgatorius*
(say: perg-a-tor-ee-us)

Lived: 65 million years ago

A changing world

Fossils show us that by 30 million years ago, the primates in Africa looked more like the great apes of today. They still lived up in trees and fruit was an important part of their diet.

Fossil Fact File

Name: *Pierolapithecus catalaunicus*
(say: peer-o-la-pith-uh-cus cat-a-lawn-i-cus)

Lived: 13 to 12.5 million years ago

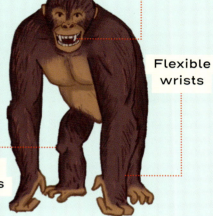

Long curved teeth

Flexible wrists

Flexible kneecaps

↑ This chimpanzee-sized primate had flexible knees and wrists, which made it good at climbing up and down trees. Gorillas, chimpanzees and humans may have all evolved from this primate.

About eight million years ago, the climate changed. The planet began to dry out and cool down. The forests across Africa shrank, giving way to grasslands and more open woodland. Fewer trees meant less fruit. Once again, it was time for primates to adapt or face extinction.

Slowly, our ancestors came down from the trees and learned to live in the new landscape. Early human fossils are found in places where there would have been a mix of habitats. Trees provided fruit, along with branches to sleep in and somewhere to hide from predators. Patches of grassland offered new foods, like roots. Rivers provided water to drink.

Around this time, the ancestors of modern humans split away from the ancestors of chimpanzees. We began evolving along different paths.

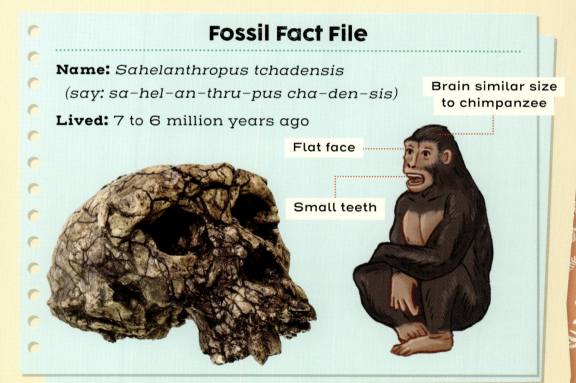

Fossil Fact File

Name: *Sahelanthropus tchadensis*
(say: sa-hel-an-thru-pus cha-den-sis)

Lived: 7 to 6 million years ago

Brain similar size to chimpanzee

Flat face

Small teeth

↑ Some scientists think this animal might have walked on two legs. However, they haven't found any body bones, so it's difficult to tell.

The first humans

Because evolution happens so slowly, it's tricky to decide when we can look at a fossil and say:

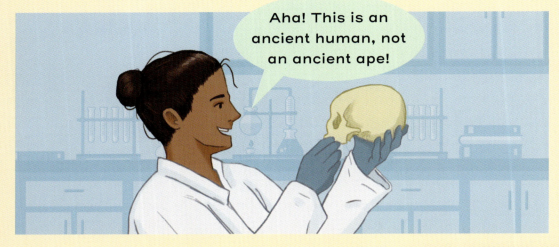

Aha! This is an ancient human, not an ancient ape!

One of the signs that scientists look for is that the animal walked on two legs. We humans are excellent walkers. Chimpanzees and gorillas can walk on two legs, but they bend their hips and knees. No other creature can match our straight-backed stride.

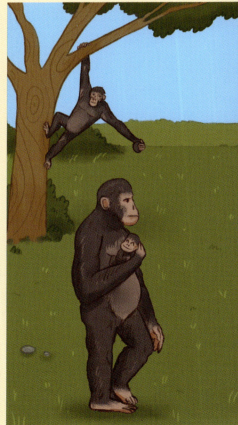

This change was probably triggered by us coming down from the trees and into the grasslands. Our ancestors might have begun to walk on two legs in order to see further into the distance to spot predators coming. It's also easier to walk on two legs when you need to keep your hands free for gathering food, carrying a baby or holding on to tools.

But it's not all about the legs. Looking at the differences between skulls is also really important for working out whether an animal might be more like an ape or more like an ancient human. Along with *Sahelanthropus tchadensis*, who you met earlier, here's another possible early human.

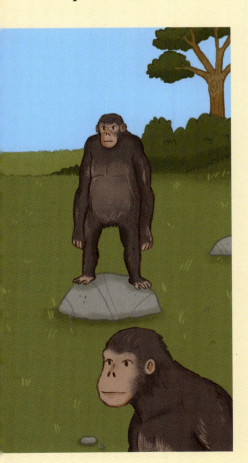

Name: *Ardipithecus ramidus*
  (say: ard-ee-pith-uh-cus ram-ee-dus)

Lived: 4.5 to 4.3 million years ago

Long arms, good for climbing

Spread big toes for grasping branches

↑ We've found lots of *Ardipithecus ramidus* fossils, including one almost complete skeleton, nicknamed Ardi. From the remains, scientists can tell that Ardi could walk around on two legs, but also that she was good at climbing trees. Her teeth show she had a mixed diet, which probably included fruits, nuts and leaves. She may also have eaten insects, eggs and small mammals.

4 Ancestors in Africa

Early human fossils have been found all over the world, but Africa is where our story began and where the oldest fossils are found. Archaeologists often look for fossils near places where our closest living relatives, chimpanzees, live today. This is because our extinct relatives probably lived in similar habitats.

Caves in South Africa have revealed hundreds of fossils. However, older human fossils have been found elsewhere.

← 'Cradle of Humankind' excavation site, South Africa. Fossils from over 3 million years ago have been found here.

Another important site is Olduvai Gorge, in Tanzania. It is in a long, deep valley, which used to be an ancient lake. The water is all dried up now, but in the layers of rock forming the valley's steep sides, many fascinating fossils have been found.

Meet Mary Leakey

Mary Leakey was born in 1913 and spent her childhood travelling around Europe. Even though women were not expected to have a career at that time, Mary dreamed of becoming an archaeologist. When she was 17, she spent some time digging up Stone Age tools in Devon, England, and was talented at illustrating them.

In 1937, Mary married Louis Leakey, a scientist and archaeologist who also shared her passion for studying ancient human life. Around ten years later, the pair began leading trips to Olduvai Gorge in Tanzania, where they soon discovered ancient fossils and tools. Among Mary's most important finds was a 1.7 million-year-old early human skull. Her many discoveries helped to prove that Africa was where the human story began.

Mary discovered this skull in 1959. →

Amazing ape-men

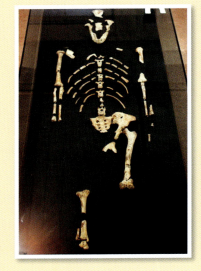

The *Australopithecines* (say: aw–struh–loh–pith–uh–seens) were an amazing group of ancient humans. Their fossils have been found all across Africa. Their name means 'Southern ape man' and we can tell they did indeed look rather ape–like from their fossils. They had long arms and round bellies, like modern chimpanzees. However, they had human features as well, and walked on two legs. A skeleton of a female *Australopithecine* was found in Ethiopia in 1974. It was nicknamed Lucy by its discoverers. Lucy may have been one of our ancestors.

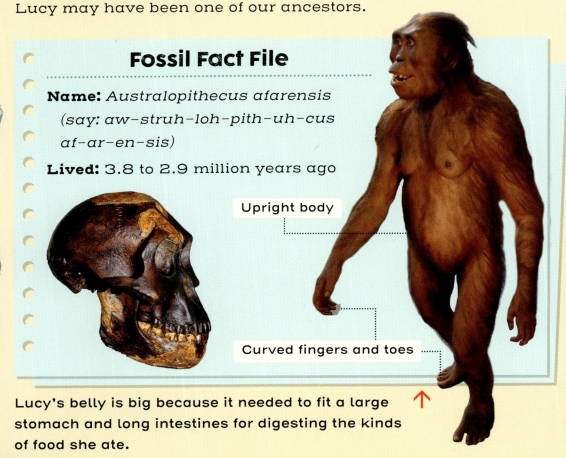

Fossil Fact File

Name: *Australopithecus afarensis* (say: aw–struh–loh–pith–uh–cus af–ar–en–sis)

Lived: 3.8 to 2.9 million years ago

Upright body

Curved fingers and toes

Lucy's belly is big because it needed to fit a large stomach and long intestines for digesting the kinds of food she ate.

Lucy was a young adult when she died. She lived in an area that would have been covered in woodland. She probably spent most of the time on the ground but may have taken shelter in the trees if she was being chased by predators.

Lucy was probably a fruit eater but she likely ate meat when she could get it. She might have scavenged the leftovers from animals killed by big cats or hyenas.

↑ A 3.3 million-year-old skeleton of the earliest child ever found in Ethiopia.

← Scientists think the earliest child discovered might have looked like this.

A different *Australopithecine* fossil was found in Dikika, Ethiopia. Nearby, archaeologists were shocked to find some animal bones that looked like the meat had been scraped off using sharp stones. This could mean that *Australopithecines* were using tools to get at their food. Scientists had thought tool use had started much later in our story, so this was a big surprise!

Forgotten footprints

In 1978, Mary Leakey's team made another amazing discovery. They came across some human-looking footprints that turned out to be about 3.6 million years old. The footprints were left in a layer of volcanic ash, which had set like concrete shortly after the footprints had been made. The footprints were probably left by the same type of early humans as Lucy. They showed that Lucy was a walker, just like us.

These footprints are a special type of fossil, known as a trace fossil. The early humans that made the tracks hadn't left any bones or teeth behind this time, but they had left a mark! It gave us a glimpse into what their lives were like.

Other early humans

Modern humans might have evolved from Lucy's species. However, other early humans have been discovered in Africa that are definitely not our direct ancestors. This next weird and wonderful early human was very odd-looking. It had a wide, flat face and very large chewing teeth.

← Footprints found in Tanzania

Fossil Fact File

Name: *Paranthropus boisei*
(say: *pah-ran-thro-pus boy-sey*)

Lived: 2.3 to 1 million years ago

Massive teeth

Powerful jaws

↑ We would have evolved from the same animal, but then adapted very differently. While our own ancestors were eating lots of different kinds of foods, these early humans only ate very tough foods, like grasses and seeds. It was a totally different kind of human to us!

5 Tools and travel

Today, we use all kinds of tools to help make our lives easier, from forks to eat our food, to hammers to build our homes. However, humans aren't the only animals that use tools.

Sea otters have a favourite rock they use to break open shells. ↓

Elephants use branches as fly swats. ↓

↑ Crows use twigs to get at food that's hard to reach.

↑ Chimpanzees make even cleverer tools. They can shape twigs into rods to scoop up termites and use sharp sticks as spears to kill prey.

What makes us special is how clever and complicated our tools can be. We have made many things to help us in lots of different situations. When archaeologists find early tools, they can begin to build a picture of how clever the humans that made them were.

Handy man

We might not know for sure if Lucy used tools, but we know a type of human that came later did. Their name was *Homo habilis*, which means 'handy man'. Thousands of stone tools have been found in areas where *Homo habilis* fossils were discovered.

Homo habilis made knives by bashing rocks ↑ against each other to create a sharp-edged stone.

Fossil Fact File

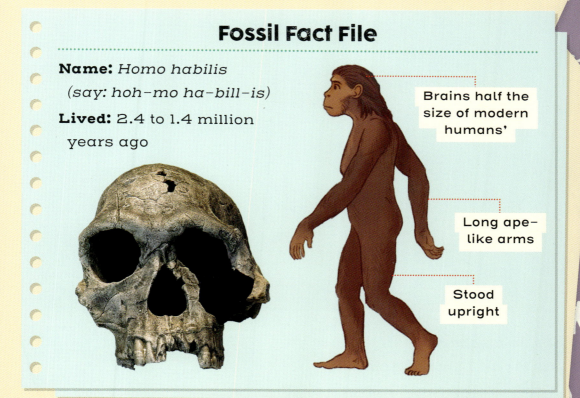

Name: *Homo habilis*
(say: hoh-mo ha-bill-is)

Lived: 2.4 to 1.4 million years ago

Brains half the size of modern humans'

Long ape-like arms

Stood upright

Early humans with strong wrists and nimble fingers were better at using tools. This meant they had a better chance of survival. They handed down these skills to their children. Over time, our ancestors became better and better tool users.

Out of Africa

Most groups of animals survive on Earth for around one million years. *Homo erectus* was a type of early human that was around for double that! Their name means 'upright man'. They were the first of our ancestors to travel out of Africa.

There were probably lots of reasons why different groups of *Homo erectus* left Africa and set off to new places. Maybe they were hunting herds of animals across the land. Perhaps they got into fights with other early humans and had to find somewhere new to live.

From fossils, we can tell they got as far as China in Asia and Spain in Europe. Somehow, they even crossed the sea to reach Indonesia. They may have been swept there by tidal waves, but it is more likely they built simple rafts and paddled over.

Spain

China

Indonesia

↑ Likely ultimate range of
Homo erectus

Fossil Fact File

Name: *Homo erectus*
  (say: *hoh-mo ee-reck-tus*)

Lived: 1.6 million to 150,000 years ago

Short arms

Long legs

↑ Early *Homo erectus* had brains that were around half the size of modern humans' brains, but later *Homo erectus* had brains nearly as big as ours.

First fires

By about one million years ago, early humans were learning to control fire. With fire, we could keep warm, scare off predators and could cook our food! This made the food easier to digest and gave us more energy. More energy meant more brain power. Fire not only made us safer, it made us smarter. By this time, early humans had created some clever tools.

Stone knives for chopping and scraping meat.

↓

Strikers to bash against stones, in order to make sharp tools.

↑

Hand axes to cut away meat and break open bones.

↓

The first artwork?

Homo erectus may have also been the world's first artist. Scientists discovered an ancient zigzag doodle scribbled on a shell, which may be 500,000 years old. This shell scribble suggests that our ancestors might have started to develop imagination and creativity.

Human hunters

Around 600,000 years ago, yet another group of early humans evolved, *Homo heidelbergensis*. These early humans used a whole new range of tools to hunt animals, including long wooden spears tipped with sharp stones. Though wood usually rots away quickly, eight 400,000-year-old spears were found in a mine in Germany. The mine's dry, dark conditions had stopped the wood rotting.

Fossil Fact File

Name: *Homo heidelbergensis*
   (say: hoh-mo high-del-burg-en-sis)
Lived: 700,000–50,000 years ago

Strong jawbone

Thick leg bones suggest they walked long distances

↑ These tall, athletic humans would have worked together to hunt and bring down prey.

Little humans

Sometimes, on islands, where food and water are limited, animals evolve to be smaller. This is because smaller animals need less to eat and drink, so have a better chance of survival! There's one island in Indonesia where this may have happened to early humans.

Fossils of a group of tiny early humans, around one metre tall, were dug up in the 2000s. When *Homo erectus* reached Indonesia, some could have got stuck on one island and evolved to be smaller. These little humans lived alongside dwarf elephants, which they hunted for food.

Fossil Fact File

Name: *Homo floresiensis*
(say: hoh-mo floor-es-ee-en-sis)
Lived: 100,000–50,000 years ago

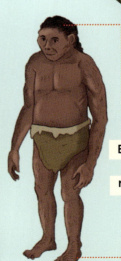

Brains about half the size of modern humans'

Long feet

↑ This cave in Indonesia is the only place where the fossils of these tiny early humans have been found.

6 Big Brains

Our brains take up just 2% of our bodies, but use 20% of our energy. If we had smaller brains, we'd need less energy. However, having big brains is what has made humans so successful. Our brains helped us develop language and live peacefully in big groups. In tricky situations, we can use our brains to come up with a plan B if our plan A goes wrong.

How the skull and brain developed over time

Australopithecus africanus

3 million years ago

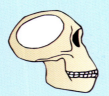

Homo erectus

750,000 years ago

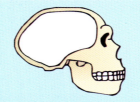

Homo neanderthalensis

400,000 years ago

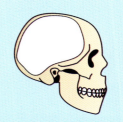

Homo sapiens

315,000 years ago to the present

Other animals have big brains. The sperm whale's brain is six times as big as ours! But compared with our body size, humans have the biggest brains on the planet. Brains don't often end up as fossils, but we can usually make a good guess at how big an animal's brain was from the size and shape of its skull, where the brain usually fits snugly.

In order to get enough energy for those big brains, early humans needed to eat a lot of food. Hunting together in groups, our ancestors had a better chance of bringing down big prey, like woolly mammoths or large deer. They could then use tools to strip and prepare the meat, before cooking it and eating it.

Big brains are brilliant, but they do have some drawbacks. We humans develop very slowly. We take a long time to grow in the womb, then when we pop out into the world, we're helpless! A baby deer can be on its hooves within hours. It can be a year or so before we take our first tottering steps or say our first words. We take twice as long to reach adulthood as chimpanzees. This is the price we pay for all our clever skills.

Long-lost relatives

One of our closest extinct relatives were the Neanderthals. Their scientific name is *Homo neanderthalensis*. When their fossils were first discovered, people thought they were foolish, clumsy cavemen. Today, scientists believe the Neanderthals might have been as clever and skilled as early *Homo sapiens*.

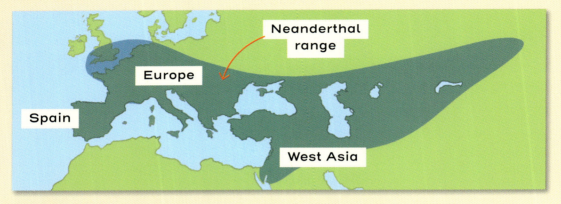

The oldest Neanderthal fossils were found in Spain, but the Neanderthals spread across much of Europe and into West Asia. Most Neanderthals were travellers, hunting across the landscape.

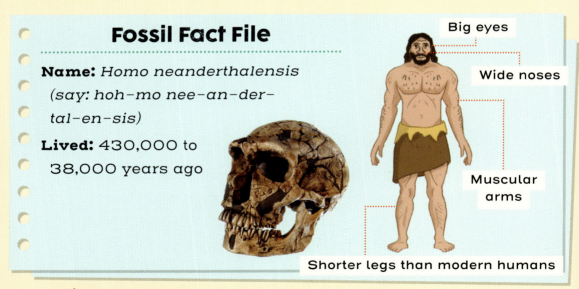

↑ Neanderthals had BIG brains – even bigger than ours. Although Neanderthals were stockier than modern humans, they were a bit bigger than us overall, so our brains are similar sizes in comparison to our bodies.

We've found a lot of Neanderthal fossils. We've also found lots of interesting clues about their way of life, from tools to ancient homes. We know that Neanderthals wore clothes and probably wore jewellery. They even left paintings on cave walls.

↑ The hole in this eagle claw suggests it could have been strung on a necklace.

← Neanderthal cave paintings

House proud

Some Neanderthals lived in caves and even split their homes into different rooms. In one cave in Italy, one chamber was used for sleeping, one for making tools and one for cutting up meat. However, the idea of Neanderthals as 'cavemen' doesn't give the full picture.

Though lots of fossils have been found in caves, some scientists think this is because predators dragged early humans into them after they died, so that they could eat them in peace!

All about language

Language is such an important part of our story – for starters, without language we wouldn't be able to tell it! Lots of other animals can communicate, but none can say quite as much as we can. For example, a monkey might have a call which means:

Leopard! Leopard!

This warns all the other monkeys that a predator is around and they need to look out!

But a human could say:

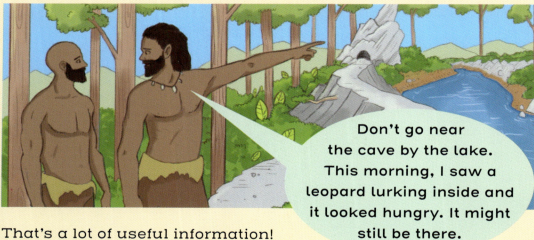

Don't go near the cave by the lake. This morning, I saw a leopard lurking inside and it looked hungry. It might still be there.

That's a lot of useful information! We can talk about things that happened in the past or might happen in the future. We can say where something happened, and when. We can be very clear and detailed.

As well as passing on information, we can pass on skills. We can explain how a tool is made and share ideas for improving it.

Though we'll never be able to find evidence of language in fossils, many scientists agree that Neanderthals could probably talk. Their language might have been simpler than ours though.

An ever-changing story

In 2010, archaeologists discovered a tiny piece of finger bone in a cave in Russia. They looked at the DNA and discovered it was from a brand-new group of humans, which scientists named the Denisovans. These humans would have lived at the same time as Neanderthals and modern humans.

Another amazing discovery was made in 2021 after scientists began to study a gigantic human skull found in China, thought to be over 146,000 years old. They believe it belonged to a kind of huge, ancient human, which they named *Homo longi*, meaning 'dragon man'. Other scientists, however, wonder if the skull might actually belong to a Denisovan ... There are still so many mysteries to solve about our past!

7 And Then There Was Us

At the same time as Neanderthals were spreading across Europe, another type of human was evolving in Africa. Scientists used to believe that all *Homo sapiens* evolved from one group in Eastern Africa. However, the ancient fossils of *Homo sapiens* have now been found all over Africa, from Morocco to South Africa. Once again, our story seems to be more complicated than was first thought.

Scientists now believe that modern humans evolved in different ways all across Africa. Some lived high up in mountains, others in grasslands and others in jungles. They all had to adapt at different times to different situations. They also had to deal with a changing climate, which flipped between cold and dry, and hot and wet.

Sometimes these conditions would bring groups of early humans together, and sometimes they would push them apart. Over thousands of years, this pattern repeated. When the groups merged, they would share ideas and sometimes have children together, passing their mixed DNA on. From this muddle, somewhere, somehow, *Homo sapiens* evolved.

But it's hard to say exactly when they evolved. Some 315,000-year-old fossils have been discovered in Morocco, which look a lot like us. However, their skulls are shaped a bit like a rugby ball, whereas ours are rounder – more like footballs! There are more fossils from around 190,000 years ago that look even more like us.

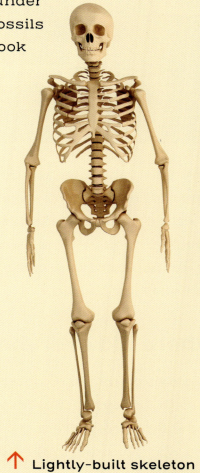

↑ Lightly-built skeleton

Fossil Fact File

Name: *Homo sapiens*
(say: hoh-mo say-pee-ens)

Lived: 315,000 years ago
to present

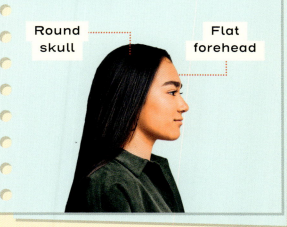

Round
skull

Flat
forehead

Humans everywhere!

Just as *Homo erectus* and other early humans had done before us, modern humans began to move out of Africa. By about 185,000 years ago, we had made it into Asia. By about 45,000 years ago, we were in Europe and Australia. By 15,000 years ago, we had crossed into the Americas. We were everywhere!

As we travelled, we would have come across other kinds of humans. We might have met *Homo erectus* in Africa and the Neanderthals in Europe. We might have bumped into the Denisovans in Asia. But within a few thousand years, the other kinds of humans had all disappeared.

Where did everybody go?

Homo sapiens lived alongside Neanderthals for up to 10,000 years. Though we probably won't ever know for sure, there are several ideas about how and why Neanderthals died out.

IDEA 1 — Killed off?

When early humans came into contact with Neanderthals, they may have killed them, forcing them to extinction.

IDEA 2 — Got too cold?

Around 40,000 years ago, there was a series of cold spells in Europe. Perhaps conditions got too bad to survive. Denisovans may have gone extinct because of the changing climate, too.

IDEA 3 — Not enough food?

When it came to competition for food, maybe *Homo sapiens* beat Neanderthals. Perhaps we were a bit faster, smarter and better adapted.

IDEA 4 — Mixed with *Homo sapiens*?

Rather than totally dying out, Neanderthals may have mixed with modern humans and had children together. Today, Europeans have up to 4% Neanderthal DNA, which supports this idea.

In parts of Asia, people have up to 6% Denisovan DNA. This might mean that *Homo sapiens* had children with Denisovans, too!

What makes us, us?

The Neanderthals disappeared around 38,000 years ago. *Homo sapiens* were the last humans left on Earth. Over the next few thousand years, we came up with the most complicated tools and inventions yet. We put our big brains to good use, making pottery, baking bread and designing bows and arrows.

Invented 20,000 years ago …

18,000 years ago …

14,500 years ago …

Sharing stories

Something very special about humans is our ability to tell stories and share ideas. We can wonder at how and why we are here. We know other animals can't do these things because they would need language to do them. To tell and understand stories, we have to be able to imagine other worlds or experiences that are outside of our everyday lives. We can also tell tales using art.

DOG DISCOVERS ANCIENT ART GALLERY

September 1940

Last Thursday, a dog named Robot tumbled down a hole in Dordogne, France while on a walk. His owner scrambled in after him and the pair made an amazing discovery! At the bottom of the tunnel, they found a cave covered with huge paintings of horses, bulls and other animals.

These paintings are about 17,000 years old – and they are not a one-off. Ancient cave art has been found on every continent except Antarctica. Our ancestors didn't just paint for fun, though. Instead, paintings were probably used to communicate. The artists might have been recording an important event that happened to their group or sharing information about where to hunt animals nearby. The paintings might even have been part of a ceremony to bring good luck on an upcoming journey.

Humans at home

At least four kinds of early humans made it to Britain.

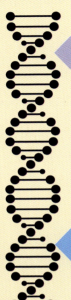

Around 900,000 years ago

A group of early humans moved through Norfolk. In 2013, their footprints were revealed by waves wearing away the rock they'd been hidden in. A few weeks later, the waves rubbed them away again.

Around 500,000 years ago

Homo heidelbergensis passed through Sussex. They left behind some fossils, along with the remains of their dinners – piles of horse, deer and rhino bones.

Around 400,000 years ago

Neanderthals hunted across Britain. Other Neanderthals returned to Britain many times, and the last evidence we have of them is from about 50,000 years ago.

Around 40,000 years ago

The first *Homo sapiens* arrived in Britain, but they didn't stay for long. Modern humans didn't settle here until the end of the last **ice age**, about 12,000 years ago.

The landscape would have been different from how it is today. Wolves, woolly mammoths, rhinos and lions roamed the land. People moved camps with the seasons and hunted for food each day.

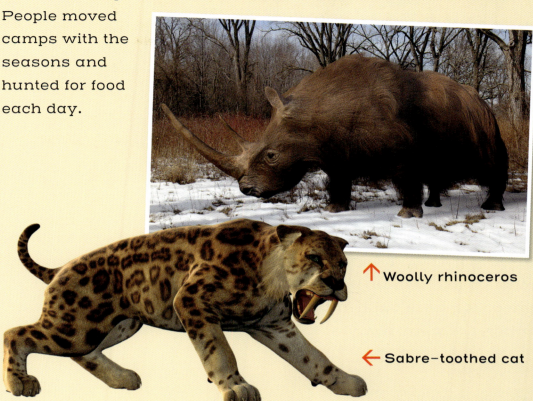

→ Woolly rhinoceros

← Sabre-toothed cat

Britain wasn't an island until around 8000–6000BCE, when rising sea levels separated it from the rest of Europe. Before that time, groups of humans could cross back and forth. Borders and countries didn't exist back then!

Settling down

For thousands of years, humans had lived by travelling from place to place. They had hunted for meat and gathered plants to eat. Farming began in the Middle East in about 10,000BCE. Rather than following herds, people kept animals for milk and meat. Instead of searching for plants, they scattered seeds and grew their own. They settled down in one place, and the first **civilisations** were born.

8 The End of Our Story?

In our short time on Earth, modern humans have made big changes. We've invented aeroplanes, books, computer games and many other amazing things. But are we still changing?

Out-of-date evolution

Some of the reactions our ancestors evolved aren't as helpful in the modern world. Our 'fight or flight' response is an automatic reaction in our brain that tells us what to do when faced with a threat. It makes our heart pound and our muscles ready to start fighting or sprint away.

↑ Fight or flight

This is great if the threat we are facing is a grumpy bear. But today, our fight or flight response sometimes kicks in at unhelpful times. It can be triggered when the threat isn't a predator, but a scary spelling test. Fighting our teacher or running away from the classroom isn't such a good idea!

What next?

Animals evolved to adapt to changes in their surroundings. Humans, however, can change their surroundings to suit them! Some scientists think this means we won't evolve any further. Most of us are lucky enough to have a warm home and enough food, and thanks to medicine and education, we are living longer than ever. For thousands of years, many humans died before they were 30 years old. But today, the average age people live to in the UK is 81.

So, perhaps *Homo sapiens* will stay the same from now on ...

However, other scientists are sure evolution will continue. In the last 150 years, the average adult height has increased by ten centimetres. Our bodies have also become better at fighting off some diseases. Though this is largely down to better diets and health care, it shows we can still adapt. So, what other ways might we change? It's unlikely our brains will get much bigger. Having bigger heads would make us topple over!

It might be that we start to use our big brains to improve ourselves using technology. Whether that means trying to change our DNA to make us healthier or putting machinery into our bodies to make us stronger, only the future will tell.

Maybe a whole new type of human will evolve! At the moment, *Homo sapiens* are the last shoot on the branch of human evolution. However, that doesn't mean that another one won't grow in the future.

Choosing to change

Whatever the distant future holds, we will need to make changes in the next few years. Today, we're facing a climate emergency. We have used too many of our planet's resources and released harmful gases into the atmosphere. We've filled our oceans with rubbish and cleared rainforests, forcing many other animals to the brink of extinction.

Just like our ancestors, we will need to put our big brains to good use to solve the problems facing us and our planet. Once again, it's time for us to adapt.

So long, sapiens

Every animal that evolves will disappear. After all, 99.9% of everything that has ever lived on Earth has now gone extinct, and one day *Homo sapiens* will, too. That won't be for a very long time though! If that seems like a sad thought, maybe try to think about it in a different way: there are so many wild and wonderful creatures that have not yet evolved that will one day walk, swim, fly or scuttle over the Earth.

So, although our time on this planet might be short, it's amazing we are here at all.

Besides, our story is not over yet!

Glossary

adapt change so that it is easier to live in a place or situation

ancestor a relative from a long time ago who a person is descended from. It can also be an early type of animal from which other animals have evolved

civilization a large, organised group of people, such as in towns and cities

DNA material in the body that carries information about how a living thing will look and act

fossil the remains or traces of ancient life

habitat a place that an animal lives

ice age a period in Earth's history when ice in the polar regions expanded because of a cooling down of the climate. Much of Europe and North America were covered in ice

predator an animal that hunts and eats other animals

primate a mammal with forward-facing eyes and grasping fingers. Monkeys, marmosets, tarsiers, lemurs, chimpanzees and humans are all primates

Index

Chat About the Book

1 Go to page 16. How do scientists identify the age of a fossil?

2 On page 5, the author invites us to 'marvel' at the mystery of our ancestors. What does 'marvel' mean?

3 Go to page 36. How does the diagram help you to understand the information about how the skull and brain developed over time?

4 Go to page 45. The author suggests 4 ways why the Neanderthals may have died out. Why has the author presented the information in this way?

5 Read page 30. How are humans similar to some kinds of animals? What makes us different?

6 Read page 28. Why is the word 'glimpse' a good word to use to describe the forgotten footprints?

7 On page 41 we learn about the discovery of the Denisovans, but what is the author's main message in this paragraph?

8 Would you like to be an archaeologist? What would you like or dislike about the job?